Contents

This is the USA!

The USA is a huge country in North America. It is divided into 50 **states**. Many people choose just one or two states to visit on their holiday.

The letters USA are short for United States of America.

These are just a few of the places you can visit in the USA!

CANADA
Great Lakes
Rocky Mountains
Chicago
New York
San Francisco
USA
Washington D.C.
Los Angeles
Florida
Pacific Ocean
MEXICO
Gulf of Mexico
Hawaii
Alaska

My Holiday in

USA

Susie Brooks

WAYLAND

First published in 2008 by Wayland

Copyright © Wayland 2008
This paperback edition published by Wayland 2012

Wayland
338 Euston Road
London NW1 3BH

Wayland Australia
Level 17/207 Kent Street
Sydney NSW 2000

Senior Editor: Claire Shanahan
Designer: Elaine Wilkinson
Map artwork: David le Jars

Brooks, Susie
My holiday in USA
1. Vacations - United States - Juvenile literature
2. Recreation - United States - Juvenile literature
3. United States - Juvenile literature 4. United States -
Social life and customs - 21st century - Juvenile
literature I. Title II. USA
917.3'04931

ISBN 978 0 7502 68240

Cover: Statue of Liberty © Bernd Obermann/Corbis; Grisly bear © Kennan Ward/Corbis.

p5: © AFP/Getty; p6: © National Geographic/Getty; p7: © Rob & Sas/Corbis; p8: © Gavin Hellier/Getty; p9: ©
Mark Peterson/Corbis; p10: © Alen MacWeeney/Corbis; p11: © Richard Cummins/Corbis; p12: © Chris Powell; p13:
© Bernd Obermann/Corbis; p14: © Getty; p15: © Kelly-Mooney Photography/Corbis; p16: © Jonathan Blair/Corbis;
p17: Lester Lefkowitz/Corbis; p18: © Jeff Hunter/Corbis; p19 Kennan Ward/Corbis; p20: © Billy Hustace/Getty;
p21: © Marilyn Angel Wynn/Nativestock Pictures/Corbis; p22: © Annie Griffiths Belt/Corbis; p23: © Jon
Feingersh/Getty; p24: ©; p25: © Sylvain Grandadam/Getty; p26, title page: © DLILLC/Corbis; p27: © Paul A.
Souders/Corbis; ©; p28: © Larry Williams/Corbis; p29: © Rob & Sas/Corbis; © Harry Rhodes/Wishlist Images
2008; p31: © Jules Frazier/Corbis.

Printed in China

Wayland is a division of Hachette Children's Books, an Hachette UK company.

www.hachette.co.uk

Each state has exciting things to see and do. You will probably fly to one of the big cities and start your adventure from there.

This is how New York looks from the aeroplane.

I felt really tired when we arrived. Mum said it was **jet lag** from the flight.

US words: at the airport

holiday
vacation

toilet
bathroom

lift
elevator

Pick a season!

The USA is so big that the weather is never the same all around the country. Usually, the hottest time to go is in summer.

Mind your feet on the scorching desert sands of Death Valley in California.

Winters are cold and snowy in many states. In the south, places near the sea are warm all year round but can have lots of rain.

The north-eastern states are famous for their bright autumn leaves. Americans call autumn 'fall'.

Weather warnings

Hot! – summer in the south
Cold! – winter in the north and the mountains
Rainy! – summer in the south-west
Windy! – spring in the **Midwest**

Best for a rest

There are lots of places to stay in the USA. Hotels range from city **skyscrapers** and roadside **motels** to quiet mountain cabins.

The Paris hotel in the lively city of Las Vegas has its own Eiffel Tower!

On a ranching holiday, you can learn to be a cowboy or cowgirl.

Camping is fun if you like being outdoors. For a real Wild West adventure, you could stay on a cattle **ranch**!

I slept really well after horseriding, but my bottom was sore the next day!

US words: packing

trainers
sneakers

trousers
pants

torch
flashlight

9

Long way to go

Journeys in the USA can be very long. The quickest way to get from state to state is by aeroplane. Some coaches and trains travel overnight.

Take something to do on long train journeys!

We were on a bus for two days. I was glad there was a loo on board!

In the past, people used to travel by boat. The rivers are still used for transport today. The Missouri is the USA's longest river.

This old-fashioned boat takes tourists along the Mississippi River.

US words: travelling

motorway
highway

railway
railroad

pavement
sidewalk

Two great cities

Washington D.C. is the capital of the USA. People come here to see where the country is ruled from, and to learn about its history.

The American President lives here in the White House, in Washington D.C.

The White House has 132 rooms, and even a bowling alley and a cinema!

New York is the USA's biggest city. Visitors love the bustling streets, bright lights, giant skyscrapers and impressive shops.

In New York, you can visit Ellis Island to see the Statue of Liberty.

New York treats

Empire State Building - look out from the 102nd floor

Yellow taxi cab - take a ride!

Central Park - for outdoor fun

Famous sights

There are other famous places that attract people to the USA. Here are just a few.

The Grand Canyon – a massive rocky valley, carved out by the Colorado River.

You can walk over the edge of the Grand Canyon on a glass bridge!

Salt Lake City – an interesting city by a lake that you can float on!

On a boat ride to Niagara, you'll hear the roar of the water and get wet in the spray.

The Niagara Falls — the second biggest waterfalls in the world.

Other popular cities

Chicago - for famous buildings

Los Angeles - home of the Hollywood movie stars

San Francisco - with a brilliant bridge

Fun breaks

Many people choose to visit a single state or region. What do you think about these?

Fantasy land (Florida)

Go wild at Walt Disney World!

Visit: Walt Disney World —
the biggest theme park ever!
SeaWorld — be a dolphin trainer and more.
Florida Keys — islands with beaches
and nature trails.

Visit: Rocky Mountains – learn to ski. Dinosaur National Monument – discover dinosaur bones. Mount Rushmore and Crazy Horse – see giant heads carved in rock.

The huge heads at Mount Rushmore show four US Presidents. Their noses are over 6 metres tall!

When we went to Hawaii, I swam with fish and saw a red-hot volcano.

17

Wild places

From **sand dunes** to volcanoes to floating icebergs, the USA has it all! People visit special **national parks** to see amazing scenery and wildlife.

In Yellowstone National Park, jets of water called geysers spurt from the ground.

In Yosemite National Park, I saw the biggest tree in the world!

Discover these

Armadillo – an animal with a bony shell

Coyote – a wolf-like wild dog

Prairie dogs – like squirrels that bark

In the centre of the USA, **bison** and **antelope** roam on grasslands called the **prairies**. In the dusty south-western deserts, there are lizards and **cacti**.

Look out for bears in the icy state of Alaska.

Meeting people

There's a wide mix of people in the USA. Many Americans came originally from other countries. You might notice the way people live or speak is different from area to area.

These children in San Francisco are celebrating Chinese New Year.

The first people to live in the USA were the Native Americans. Their lives changed when people from Europe took over the country.

A few Native Americans still live like they used to. Many speak their own languages.

Native American living

tipi (tee-pee) - a cone-shaped tent
wigwam/wickiup - a dome-shaped hut
pow-wow - a traditional ceremony

Feasts of food

Hamburgers, salads, apple pies...
whatever you eat in the USA,
expect it to be BIG! The choice
is enormous too — you'll find
food from all over the world.

Eating at a
resturant is fun.
You can try food
you've never
had before.

In the USA, chips are called fries
and crisps are called chips.

Barbecues are popular in summer. Try meat kebabs with pineapple rings!

People cook differently from state to state. In Maine, for example, seafood is popular, while Texas is known for great steaks.

On the menu

Peanut butter and jelly (jam) sandwich

Gumbo - a soup or stew with rice

Twinkie - sponge cake filled with cream

Shop till you drop!

Some people go to the USA just for the shopping! In New York, you can buy almost anything – as long as you have some dollars to spend and lots of time to look around.

New York has some of the biggest shops in the world! This is Toys R Us in New York.

Look for **souvenirs** to take home. Many Native Americans sell their homemade crafts to tourists.

This Native American lady makes colourful woven rugs and mats to sell in her shop.

I bought a Mickey Mouse toy to remind me of Disney World.

US words: shopping

shopping centre
mall

shop
store

queue
line

A big game

Watching a baseball or American football match is exciting in the USA. Everyone screams for their favourite team! Basketball is popular, too.

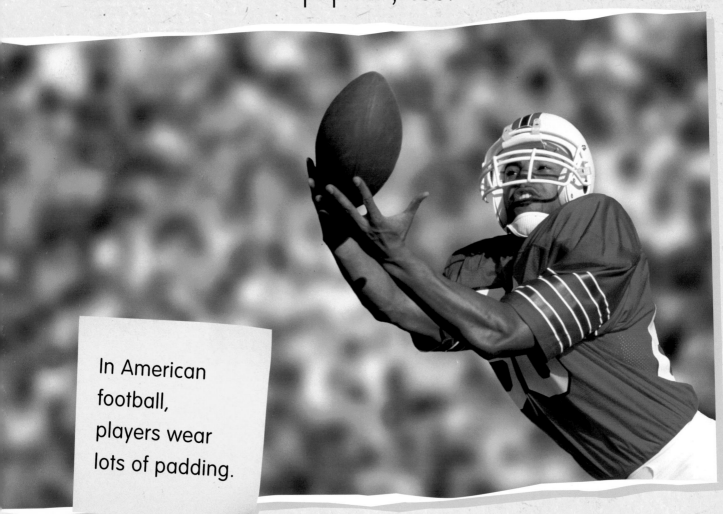

In American football, players wear lots of padding.

During the baseball game, we cheered so much I nearly lost my voice!

People go to Hawaii to surf on gigantic waves.

You can try all sorts of sports in the countryside, including mountain biking, rock climbing, horseriding and white water rafting.

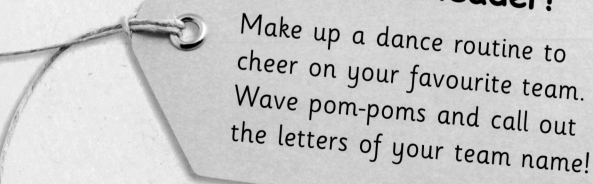

Be a cheerleader!

Make up a dance routine to cheer on your favourite team. Wave pom-poms and call out the letters of your team name!

Happy holidays

If you visit the USA late in November, get ready for Thanksgiving. On the fourth Thursday of the month, families meet up and enjoy a tasty feast.

Thanksgiving foods include turkey, potatoes and pecan or pumpkin pie.

I ate so much on Thanksgiving, I thought I was going to pop!

Cat, witch, ghost or spook...you can dress up and join in the fun on Halloween!

Other festivals happen throughout the year.
On Halloween children go trick-or-treating.
At Mardi Gras there are colourful parades.

Festivals to catch

Easter Monday	4th July	Christmas	
roll eggs on the White House lawn	Independence Day fireworks and parades	see New York's spectacular tree	

Make it yourself

At traditional Native American celebrations, people dance to the beat of drums. Make this drum to play at your own pow-wow!

Pow-wow drum

You will need:

- a round tin or tub
- brown paper
- scissors
- PVA glue and brush
- sticky tape
- coloured paper.

1. Cut a circle of brown paper big enough to cover the top of the tin and fold over the sides.

2. Paint the paper circle with PVA glue and let it dry. Do this twice.

3. Stretch the paper over the tin's opening and tape it around the sides.

4. Tear strips of coloured paper and glue them around your drum.

TIP: You could cut animal shapes out of magazines to stick on your drum.

5. Decorate with paper shapes or even feathers and string.

6. Beat your drum with a chopstick or wooden spoon.

Useful words

antelope   A long-legged, deer-like animal.

bison   A shaggy, cow-like animal, also known as a buffalo.

cacti   Prickly plants that grow in deserts.

jet lag   Feeling tired or sick after a long flight.

Midwest   The north-central part of the USA.

motel   A roadside hotel for drivers to stop at.

national park   A protected part of the countryside that people can visit.

prairies   Grassy lands in the central USA, also called the Great Plains.

ranch   A big farm with lots of land for cattle or other animals to graze on.

sand dunes   Large mounds of drifted sand.

skyscraper   A very tall building with many floors.

souvenir   Something you take home to remind you of somewhere you have been.

state   A region of the USA. Each state has its own capital city. The biggest state is Alaska. Hawaii is an island state.